KIDS IN PIONEER TIMES

Lisa A. Wroble

The Rosen Publishing Group's
PowerKids Press™
New York

Published in 1997 by The Rosen Publishing Group, Inc.
29 East 21st Street, New York, NY 10010

First Edition

Book Design: Danielle Primiceri

Photo Credits: Cover, pp. 4, 8, 16, 20 © Corbis-Bettmann; pp. 11, 12 © The Bettmann Archive; pp. 7, 15, 19 © Bettmann.

Wroble, Lisa A.
     Kids in pioneer times / Lisa A. Wroble.
          p.   cm.—(Kids throughout history)
     Includes index.
     ISBN 0-8239-5119-7
     1. Pioneer children—West (U.S.)—Juvenile literature. 2 Frontier and pioneer life—West (U.S.)—Juvenile literature. 3. West (U.S.)—Social life and customs—Juvenile literature. I. Title. II. Series.
     F596.W76 1997
     978'.02'083—dc21   96-37835
                                                                                          CIP
                                                                                          AC

Manufactured in the United States of America

CONTENTS

SETTLING IN THE WEST

Pioneers (py-uh-NEERZ) were the early settlers of the western part of the United States. By the year 1760, there was no land left to farm in the original thirteen **colonies** (KOL-un-eez). Many people decided to head west to find more land. Pioneers often traveled together in wagon trains. They brought only what they needed to **survive** (ser-VYV): farming and building tools, seeds for planting, clothes, and food for the trip.

◀ *Pioneer families traveled hundreds or even thousands of miles to find land on which to farm and build.*

FRONTIER LIFE

Paul's family settled on the **frontier** (frun-TEER) in what is now South Dakota. It was a long **journey** (JER-nee). There were no roads. The lead, or head, wagon made the trail for everyone as it traveled. Finally, the families decided to stop on some beautiful land and they built their houses and farms. First, the pioneers had to clear the land of trees so they could plant crops. Growing food was more important than building houses. People camped out until the plowing and planting were done.

Pioneers camped out during their journey and once they reached their new land. ▶

BUILDING A HOME

The trees that were cleared from the fields were used to build log cabins. Everyone in the wagon train helped to build each house. Men cut notches at the ends of the logs so they would fit together. Paul and his sister, Mary, stuffed clay, moss, and mud in the gaps between the logs. This helped keep the cabin warm and dry. The roof was made from wide, flat planks of wood. There was a dirt floor covered with wooden boards. The door was made of thick planks hung with leather hinges.

Most pioneers built log cabins using the trees that they had cleared from the land to plant crops.

LIVING IN A LOG CABIN

Paul and Mary slept in a loft above the kitchen. They shared a mattress made of canvas and filled with dried leaves. It rested on two thick logs, which raised it off the floor. Their clothes hung on pegs along the wall. Paul and Mary used a ladder to climb up and down from their loft. Their father made the table and benches in the kitchen near the fireplace. They were made of split logs and had sturdy legs. The fireplace was large with a stone **hearth** (HARTH). It was used for cooking meals and warming the cabin.

Most pioneer families made all of their own furniture. ▶

CHORES

Before breakfast, Paul fed the farm animals and brought in wood for the fire. Mary gathered eggs from the chicken coop. She helped her mother fry them and make corn cakes for breakfast. After breakfast, Paul ground corn into meal, helped his father in the fields, and helped make soap. Mary milked the cow and helped churn, or make, butter. Mary and her mother also grew a plant called flax to spin into yarn and weave into linen cloth. Sheep fleece was also spun and woven into wool cloth.

◀ *Every member of the family had chores to do.*

13

CLOTHES

Mary and her mother made the clothes for the family. Women and girls wore wool dresses, **petticoats** (PET-ee-cohts), and aprons or smocks. When it was cold, they wore shawls over their shoulders. Women and girls wore **bonnets** (BON-ets) with wide brims to hide their faces and necks from the sun. Paul and his father wore pants and long shirts made out of deerskin. During the winter, Paul wore a hat made from the fur of a raccoon he had caught. During the summer, he and his father wore straw hats.

Pioneers wore clothes made from plants they grew and animals they caught. ▶

FOOD

Corn and meat were the foods that pioneers ate most. Corn could be roasted or used to make other dishes, such as porridge and corn bread. The pioneers ate beans, potatoes, and squash that they grew. They raised cattle, hogs, sheep, and chickens, and hunted deer, turkeys, buffalo, and rabbits. It was hard to keep food fresh. To keep meat from spoiling, Paul's mother dried strips in the sun, smoked them over a fire, or soaked them in salt. She used honey, molasses, maple syrup, and maple sugar to make foods sweet.

Pioneers often ate stews made with meat and vegetables. Stews were made in one pot and were easy to cook.

WORK AND PLAY

Frontier life was so busy that pioneers found ways to mix work and play. Women had **quilting bees** (KWIL-ting BEEZ). Families got together to gather nuts or **harvest** (HAR-vest) crops. Corn-husking parties were often held. Teams raced to see who could peel their pile of corn first. Maple sugaring parties were held in early spring. Small holes were made in maple trees, and the sap was caught in buckets. Everyone helped boil the sap into syrup and sugar. These work parties ended with great feasts.

Pioneers worked hard, but they also had fun singing, dancing, and playing instruments such as the fiddle and the harmonica. ▶

EDUCATION

Until there were enough people to make up a small town, no schools or churches were built. Instead, parents taught their children the skills they needed. Paul learned to use an ax and a rifle, to care for farm animals, and to make and fix tools. Mary learned to cook, spin, weave, and sew. On Sundays, people gathered at one family's house. The mother or father of that family would read from the Bible. Children learned the alphabet and their numbers by looking at the Bible.

After many pioneer families had settled in one area, they built a school and a church.

HELPING EACH OTHER

The pioneers left their friends and families when they headed west. Each family **relied** (ree-LYD) on the other families in the wagon train. To survive the long, hard journey, they had to help each other. There were no doctors around. If someone was sick, the women made medicine from herbs, roots, and tree bark. When one family ran out of food, the others shared theirs. They helped each other farm and build. The pioneers became a strong, close **community** (kuh-MYOO-nih-tee).

GLOSSARY

bonnet (BON-et) A covering for the head usually tied under the chin with strings or ribbons.

colonies (KOL-un-eez) The early British settlements that became the United States.

community (kuh-MYOO-nih-tee) A group of people living together.

frontier (frun-TEER) The last edge of settled country, where the wilderness begins.

harvest (HAR-vest) To pick and gather food grown on farms.

hearth (HARTH) The stone or brick floor of a fireplace.

journey (JER-nee) A long trip.

petticoat (PET-ee-coht) A skirt worn under a dress.

pioneer (py-uh-NEER) A person who settles in a part of a country, getting it ready for others to move there.

quilting bee (KWIL-ting BEE) People who gather together to sew a bed covering made of cloth sewn over soft padding.

rely (ree-LY) To depend on or trust.

survive (ser-VYV) To keep living.

 INDEX